11/14

COMMUNITY · CONNECTIONS

?

GETTING TO KNOW OUR PLANET
SAHARA DESERT

BY VICKY FRANCHINO

CHERRY
LAKE
Publishing

Published in the United States of America by Cherry Lake Publishing
Ann Arbor, Michigan
www.cherrylakepublishing.com

Content Adviser: Linda Hooper-Bùi, PhD, Associate Professor, Department of
Environmental Science, Louisiana State University Agricultural Center, Baton Rouge, Louisiana
Reading Adviser: Marla Conn, Read With Me Now

Photo Credits: Cover and page 1, © sunsinger/Shutterstock.com; page 5, © Daniel Gilbey
Photography - My portfolio/Shutterstock.com; page 7, © ANDRZEJ GRZEGORCZYK/
Shutterstock.com; page 9, © Anton_Ivanov/Shutterstock.com; page 11, © Denis Burdin/
Shutterstock.com; page 13, © Pichugin Dmitry/Shutterstock.com; page 15,
© Sukpaiboonwat/Shutterstock.com; page 17, © Vladimir Wrangel/Shutterstock.com;
page 19, © cdrin/Shutterstock.com; page 21, © posztos/Shutterstock.com.

LIBRARY OF CONGRESS CATALOGING-IN-PUBLICATION DATA
Names: Franchino, Vicky, author.
   Title: Sahara Desert / by Vicky Franchino.
Other titles: Community connections (Cherry Lake Publishing)
Description: Ann Arbor, Michigan : Cherry Lake Publishing, [2016] |
   Series: Community connections | Series: Getting to know our planet |
   Audience: K to grade 3. |
   Includes bibliographical references and index.
Identifiers: LCCN 2015039841| ISBN 9781634705189 (lib. bdg.) |
   ISBN 9781634705783 (pdf) | ISBN 9781634706384 (pbk.) |
   ISBN 9781634706988 (ebook)
Subjects: LCSH: Sahara—Juvenile literature. | Desert people—Africa—
   Juvenile literature. | Desert animals—Africa—Juvenile literature.
Classification: LCC DT334 .F73 2016 | DDC 916.6—dc23 LC record available
at http://lccn.loc.gov/2015039841

Cherry Lake Publishing would like to acknowledge the
work of The Partnership for 21st Century Skills. Please
visit www.p21.org for more information.

Printed in the United States of America
Corporate Graphics
January 2016

SAHARA DESERT

CONTENTS

GETTING TO KNOW OUR PLANET

ENORMOUS AND DRY

Imagine a place where the sun is hot. The air is dry. There is little else but sand and rocks in every direction. This is the Sahara Desert. This desert is in North Africa. It covers 3.5 million square miles (9.1 million square kilometers). That's huge! Most of the United States could fit inside it!

The Sahara Desert stretches across most of Northern Africa.

The Sahara Desert is the world's largest hot desert. Only the cold Arctic and Antarctic deserts are bigger. What do you already know about the Sahara Desert? What questions do you hope this book will answer?

Deserts get very little **precipitation**. Just think about the Sahara's yearly rainfall. Most of the desert gets less than 5 inches (12.7 centimeters). It is very hot much of the time, too. Daytime temperatures are often at least 120 degrees Fahrenheit (49 degrees Celsius). At night, the temperature can be close to freezing.

People who live in the desert must be careful about water. They need a good supply for themselves and their animals.

Windstorms are common in the desert. The wind carries dirt and sand for miles. During these storms, it is almost impossible to see. How could you protect yourself in a windstorm? How could you find your way somewhere?

NOT JUST SAND DUNES

Sand dunes are very common in the Sahara. These are hills of sand formed by the wind. You might think the Sahara is completely filled with sand. It's not! Much of the desert is made up of gravel. There are also rocky plains and mountains. The highest point is Mount Koussi. It is more than 11,000 feet (3,353 meters) high.

Some parts of the Sahara have more rock or gravel than sand.

Have you seen a sand dune? Look at some pictures in books or online. Sand dunes are not just in the desert. They're also common at the edges of bodies of water. Sand dunes come in many different shapes and sizes.

Most of the Sahara is very dry. But there are special places where there is water. These are called **oases**. Animals and people visit an oasis for water to drink. Dates, figs, olives, citrus fruits, and grains grow here. Most people living in the Sahara live near an oasis.

Trees, grasses, and other plants sprout up in oases.

A **mirage** is a trick of the desert. A mirage makes it look like there's a pool of water. But the place is really only sand. What do you think might cause this to happen?

11

ADAPTABLE SURVIVORS

The Sahara might seem like a difficult place to live. However, many animals have **adapted** to the desert. They can survive hot temperatures and need very little water. A camel can go for a week without drinking water! It also has a hump on its back. This hump stores fat. The fat provides energy when there is little to eat.

Camels are one of the most well-known animals in the Sahara.

Animals in the Sahara deal with extreme heat and cold. Some animals burrow into the earth. Others are **nocturnal**. They only come out at night. Can you guess how these activities help the animals survive?

13

The fennec fox has huge ears. They help release heat from the fox's body. This keeps the fox cool. The dorcas gazelle doesn't have to search for water to drink. The plants it eats provide all the moisture the gazelle needs.

A fennec fox's light-colored fur helps it blend in with its sandy surroundings.

Desertification means a desert is growing bigger. Can you think of what could cause a desert to grow? Is there anything that people can do to stop desertification?

The Sahara has many lizards and snakes. You'll also find frogs, toads, snails, shrimp, and even crocodiles near water. Hundreds of types of birds spend time in the Sahara. Some **migrate** there for the winter or summer. Others stay all year. One bird that stays is the ostrich. It is the world's largest bird.

The Sahara Desert is home to a range of insects.

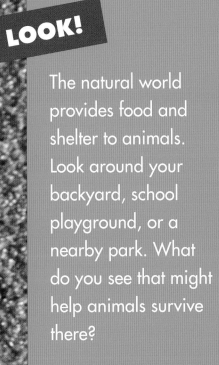

LOOK!

The natural world provides food and shelter to animals. Look around your backyard, school playground, or a nearby park. What do you see that might help animals survive there?

NOMADIC PEOPLE

Some people who live in the Sahara are **nomads**. They move from place to place. Many of them raise goats, sheep, or cattle. They move to find grass for their animals. Nomads live in tents. These tents are easy to pack up and carry. The nomads sleep during the hottest part of the day. They always travel with a supply of water.

A nomad's tent can be put up or taken down in little time.

THINK!

People in the desert often wear clothes over their entire bodies. That may seem like it would be hot. What do you think are the benefits of dressing this way?

19

The Sahara Desert isn't an easy place to live. Fewer than three million people make their home there. This is only about one person for every 1 square mile (2.6 sq km). But the Sahara can be quite beautiful. Imagine seeing a sunrise over an ocean of sand! Would you like to live in the Sahara?

A woman walks with her herd of animals.

Use what you've learned about the Sahara to create art. Draw sand dunes or the animals and people of the desert. Or paint a beautiful oasis. You could even add real sand or rock. Use your imagination!

GLOSSARY

adapted (uh-DAPT-ed) made something work in a different way or for a different use

desertification (dez-urt-i-fi-KAY-shun) when land loses its water, vegetation, and wildlife and becomes a desert

migrate (MYE-grate) to move to another area or climate at a specific time of year

mirage (muh-RAHZH) a trick of the eye caused by air and weather conditions that makes something appear to be there that isn't

nocturnal (nahk-TUR-nuhl) active at night

nomads (NOH-madz) members of a community that travel from place to place instead of living in one place

oases (oh-AY-seez) places in the desert where there's water and trees and plants can grow

precipitation (pre-sip-i-TAY-shuhn) when water falls from the sky as rain, sleet, hail, or snow

FIND OUT MORE

BOOKS

Bailey, Gerry. *Dry in the Desert*. New York: Crabtree Publishing, 2013.

Lappi, Megan. *Sahara Desert: The World's Largest Desert*. New York: AV2 Books, 2014.

WEB SITES

Conservation Institute: 9 Interesting Facts About the Sahara Desert
www.conservationinstitute.org/interesting-sahara-desert-facts
Discover nine interesting facts about the Sahara Desert!

YouTube—National Geographic
www.youtube.com/watch?v=nDWpFlt3xK4
Travel along with the National Geographic crew as they learn more about life in the Sahara.

INDEX

24

ABOUT THE AUTHOR

Vicky Franchino thinks it's a lot of fun to learn about new things, and she especially likes learning about new places. Vicky has visited deserts in the United States but has never seen a desert as big as the Sahara. She would be a little nervous to travel someplace where it is so hot and there isn't very much water— she would rather visit an oasis! Vicky lives with her family in Wisconsin, where there is usually plenty of water.